# PORT GAMBLE

More Than A Bend In The Road

History of A Pacific Northwest Lumber Town

CHRISTOPHER J. FOX

**Port Gamble**: More Than a Bend in the Road /
　　　　　　　History of a Pacific Northwest Lumber Town

Published by:

Bad Burro Press, an imprint of
Catalyst Publications, Inc.
PO Box 2485, Kirkland, WA 98083-2485

catalystpublicationsinc.com

Printed in the United States of America
First Printing 2020

ISBN 978-1-943783-17-5

# CONTENTS

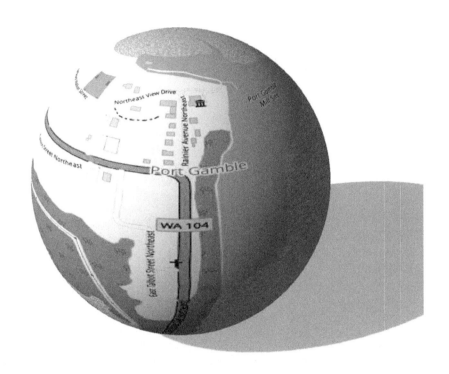

## Port Gamble, Washington

Latitude: 47°51'15.34"N

Longitude: 122°35'1.53"W

# FOREWORD

Port Gamble, Kitsap County, State of Washington, may seem at first glance to be just a quaint town at a bend in the road (Highway 104). But first impressions are deceiving. Slow your pace, resist the urge to pass by, and draw back the curtain on the town's calm, well-restored exterior. Discoveries await.

This book explores the history and stories of Port Gamble through photographs, vintage news articles and historical archives. Although there are local reports of paranormal activities, Port Gamble is far from a ghost town. It has a very vibrant and intriguing past, beginning with the S'Klallam, Twana (Skokomish), Chemakum (Chimakum or Chimacum), and Suquamish tribes, and continuing through the following centuries with East Coast entrepreneurs and today's inhabitants and retailers.

The Port Gamble Historic District, a National Historic Landmark, was the site of the longest operating lumber mill in the United States until it closed in 1995 with many structures removed two years later. Founded in 1853 by Andrew Pope and Captain William Talbot from East Machias, Maine, the approximately 300 acre property is currently managed by the Olympic Property Group on behalf of Pope Resources. A two year remedial project, completed in 2017, cleaned up over 106 acres of Port Gamble Bay, including the removal of 8,592 pilings and 1.3 acres of over-water structures and docks.

The area is home to a variety of birds, including great blue herons, ospreys and cormorants. Within the 65 acre town site there is a community store, a post office, a performance theater, a historical museum, an outdoor activity business, antique stores, restaurants, and more.

Looking forward in time, extensive development plans have been proposed and are under consideration by the Kitsap County Department of Community Development.

Port Gamble is a place of interest and importance: past, present and future. *Christopher J. Fox*

Artwork on sign at S'Kallam's Little Boston  park
overlooking Point Julia and Port Gamble Bay
*Artist Unknown*

*Chapter I*

# S'KLALLAM NATION

Long before the arrival of people of European descent, the region around Port Gamble was home to indigenous societies, including the S'Klallam, Twana (Skokomish), Chemakum (Chimakum or Chimacum), and Suquamish Tribes. The S'Klallam, called the Nux Sklai Yem, *Strong People*, belonged to the Salish speaking people whose history in the Puget Sound basin dates to before 1400 A.D.

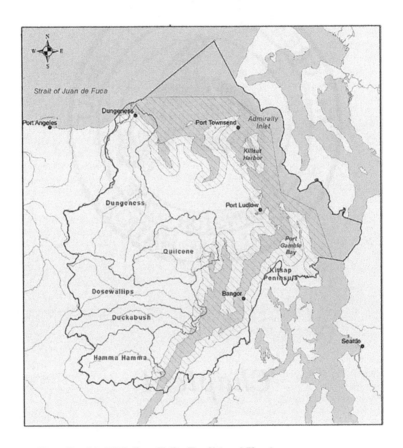

**Port Gamble S'Klallam Tribe Traditional Use Area.**

*Projections of Future Transitions in Tidal Wetlands under Sea Level Rise within the Port Gamble S'Klallam Traditional Use Areas.* Mary F. Ramirez and Charles A. Simenstad, School of Aquatic and Fishery Sciences, University of Washington. January, 2018

2

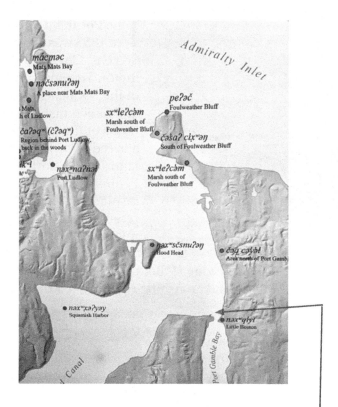

In 1853, Joseph Keller, an employee of San Francisco's Pope and Talbot, filed a "donation claim" on the land occupied by the S'Kallam. He offered the S'Kallams incentives to move from the intended lumber mill site to Little Boston at Point Julia, east across the bay. The mill supplied lumber to build houses, a school and a church. Tribe members worked at the mill and shopped at its store while selling fish and clams to the settlers.

Today the Port Gamble S'Klallam Reservation encompasses approximately 1,700 acres of land held in trust by the federal government. The Tribe presently has approximately 1,200 enrolled members.

For further information about the history and culture of the area's native populations, readers are referred to *Native Peoples of the Olympic Peninsula, by the Olympic Peninsula Intertribal Cultural Advisory Committee.* Edited by Jacilee Wray. University of Oklahoma Press. 2002

3

The **Point No Point Treaty** of 1855 was signed by Isaac Stevens, Governor of Washington Territory, and leaders of the S'Kallam, Chimakum and Skokomish Tribes. By terms of the treaty, the Indians ceded ownership of their lands on the northern Kitsap Peninsula and Olympic Peninsula in exchange for small reservations, $60,000 and retention of fishing rights.

Federal District Court Judge H. Boldt, in his 1974 landmark decision reaffirming the Indian fishing rights, noted that the treaty was

"written in English, a language unknown to most of the tribal representatives, and translated by an interpreter in the service of the United States using Chinook Jargon, which was also unknown to some tribal representatives. Having only about three hundred words in its vocabulary, the Jargon was capable of conveying only rudimentary concepts, but not the sophisticated or implied meaning of treaty provisions about which highly learned jurists and scholars differ."

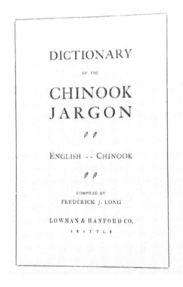

DICTIONARY

OF THE

CHINOOK JARGON

ENGLISH -- CHINOOK

COMPILED BY
FREDERICK J. LONG

LOWMAN & HANFORD CO.
SEATTLE

# sɫə́ŋct st

## We are still here (we persevere)

It is important to remember it was our ancestors that never became faint of heart, never gave up on their protests about unfairness of treaty promises not kept by the U.S. government, and never left our lands where our dead were buried. We can be proud of how we survived and carried on the values and traditions of the 'Strong People'."

Ron Charles, former Port Gamble S'Kallam Chairman

On exhibit at
**The Point - Casino & Hotel**
7989 Salish Lane NE
Kingston, WA 98346
*thepointcasinoandhotel.com*

# tiə cəʔít skʷáčiɫ

## Our Natural World (genuine world)

The S'Klallam language, knowledge and livelihood came for our surrounding natural world. "Both before and during treaty times, S'Klallam families' lives revolve around the seasons...[we] gathered berries, roots, medicinal plants, and other foods and materials during our regular season travels. S'Klallam children learned early on that all of life was connected and that the bounty of food provided by nature occurs in cycles."

From 'The Strong People; A history of the Port Gamble S'Klallam Tribe

*Chapter II*

# HISTORIC
# PORT GAMBLE

## William C. Talbot
### 1816-1861

In July 1853, Captain William C. Talbot (1816-1881), together with Andrew Pope established the steam sawmill Puget Mill Co. at Port Gamble.

Ten men constructed a bunkhouse, cookhouse, and store before starting work on the mill. The site was on a sand spit the local Native Americans called Teekalet, meaning "brightness of the noonday sun." The name was later changed to Port Gamble in 1868. The mill operated continuously for 142 years, from 1853 to 1995.

Source: Edwin T. Coman, Jr. and Helen M. Gibbs,
*Time, Tide and Timber: A Century of Pope & Talbot*
(Stanford, CA: Stanford University Press, 1949), 51-61, 74-77

# The Late Captain Talbot

William Chaloner Talbot, whose sudden death at Astoria was announced by telegraph on Saturday, has so long been connected with the commercial interest of San Francisco as to deserve more than a passing notice.

He was born at East Machias, Maine, February 28, 1816. He came to California around Cape Horn, in command of the brig Oriental, in 1849, arriving in the spring of 1850. In the summer of 1853 he went to Washington Territory and established Lumber Mills at Teekalet, now Port Gamble, on Puget Sound. Later on he bought other mills at Utsalady and Port Ludlow, Washington Territory. These towns have largely been built up under the thrift of lumber interests. The last six weeks of his life were passed most pleasantly by him, in company with several members of his household and other friends, in this locality. As late as last Sunday morning telegrams were sent from Portland, Oregon to friends in this city, announcing the fact of their sailing on the Columbia that day for San Francisco, and saying that all were well. About 5 o'clock the same day a telegram from Astoria announced the sudden death at that point of Captain Talbot. He died of heart disease.

Captain Talbot was in the full plenitude of his powers, active, earnest, yet always placid and genial. He possessed rare qualities of mind and heart. He was a firm friend, affectionate and tender in his family relations and a devoted husband and father. He amassed a large fortune, with which he aided in the building up of the great commercial interests of the Pacific coast. The lumber trade of this coast has been for years very largely in the hands of Messrs. Pope & Talbot.

Mr. Talbot gave liberally for the sustaining of local charities and was still better pleased to aid the worthy. Although so active and devoted to business cares and duties, Captain Talbot took special delight in the study of ethical and scientific subjects. He was a full man, with a well-furnished and disciplined mind. His extensive travel, both in this country and in Europe, had made him cosmopolitan in spirit and in temper. He was reverent and religious of soul, but thoroughly unsectarian in tendency. In the death of Captain Talbot, San Francisco has lost a valued citizen and this coast has lost one of its most enterprising men. He leaves a wife and five children, two sons and three daughters.

*Daily Intelligencer.* Wednesday, August 17, 1881

# Lt. Robert Gamble

Wounded in War of 1812
aboard the frigate,
USS President.

# USS President

Launched in 1800, this 44
gun three-masted frigate
joined the fledgling US
Navy to protect American
merchant ships.

In 1856 a large numer of northern Haida tribe members approached Port Gamble in war canoes. The locals took shelter in a blockhouse. The USS Massachusetts arrived and landed a shore party on November 21, 1856. During the ensuing battle twenty-five natives and one sailor, Gustav Englebrecht, were killed. Englebrecht, the first US Navy man killed in the Pacific, is buried at the Buena Vista Cemetery in Port Gamble.

Original octagonal blockhouse.

The site was later occupied by a blacksmith shop.

# PORT GAMBLE, Sept. 15, 1882

Leaving Seabeck, I returned to Port Gamble where I spent a few days quite pleasantly. I had the good fortune to fall in with an old California friend, Dr. J.A. Martin, formerly Superintendent of Public Schools of Los Angeles County, with whom the time not engaged in interviewing people for "notes to print," was pleasantly spent in recalling memories of our old home. The Doctor has happened upon a flourishing practice in Port Gamble and the adjacent county and may be relied upon by our neighbors to lend valuable assistance in their educational matters whenever he is called upon to do so.

**Port Gamble** is historically interesting. Known in its earlier days as Teekalet, an Indian name which may be translated freely as "the place for throwing the dips," hence it was a greatly gambling place for the aborigines. It was chosen early in the 50's as the site of one of the large lumbering mills for which Puget Sound is famous, the world over.

**The Location** of Port Gamble is a pleasant one, on a bay of ample dimensions at a point where Hood's Canal and Admiralty Inlet meet and mingle their waters. The business of the mill exclusively has built up a thriving town of several hundred inhabitants. Many of the residences are well and ornamentally built and are fairly embowered in fruit trees and shrubbery. Flowers of almost endless variety lend a home-like charm to the front yards and the occupants of these homes show that they know how to mingle the useful with the beautiful by planting and successfully cultivating all varieties of berries and small fruits.

**The Fraternal Orders** are represented by flourishing Lodges of Masons, Odd Fellows and the United Order of Workmen. A presentable church building, located on the hill back of the mill site, is a pleasant reminder of a due regard for the better influences which operate on the minds and consciences of man, and a comfortable school house with a large attendance bears witness in the same direction.

**The Headquarters** for a long time of the extensive operations of the Puget Mill Company, embracing Port Gamble, Port Ludlow and Utsalady, the site of the company has grown into a wholesale establishment of large proportions, and the stock carried embraces almost everything which the multifarious wants of the community could suggest, form a spool of the finest sewing cotton to a chain fit for the right bower of an East India merchantman.

**A Vast Landed Domain**, variously estimated from the lower figures up to 500,000 acres, is to be reckoned among the possessions of the company, as well as a fleet of lumber ships, barks and barkentines, and four of the most power tugs on the Sound.

**At the Teekalet Hotel**, Mr. John Collins, of Seattle, proprietor, and Mrs. James McGraw, manager, assisted by an old Swedish gentleman, whose name, I am sorry to say, has escaped my memory, I found pleasant quarters, a comfortable room and clean linen on the bed; in addition to which I received attentions which a sick man were very grateful, for which I desire to return my thanks.

A.T.H.

*Seattle Daily Post-Intelligencer.* October 1, 1882

**Port Gamble. Sept. 1** - The Republican convention met here yesterday for the purpose of electing delegates to the state convention, the organizing of a new cental committee and nominating the officers to be elected this fall. The usually quiet town was agog with excitement, and the halls of the old Teekalet hotel rang with the shrill whisper of the wirepuller.

*The Seattle Post-Intelligencer.* Sept. 2, 1898

15

Port Gamble (Puget Mill Company) is the largest milling corporation on Puget Sound, (Pope Talbot, San Francisco) and Mr. Cyrus Walker is resident manager at Gamble. Last year the Gamble company cut over 30,000,000 feet of lumber, the year being a dull one. The average number of men employed about the mill is 160. The new mill contains one circular, two gangs, one table edge, two gangs of edgers, one lath mill, six trimmers, two planing machines.

*The Vancouver Independent.* January 27, 1881

*Source: History of the Pacific Northwest: Oregon and Washington, F852 .H67 1889 v.2 c.2 at Washington State University Libraries' Manuscripts, Archives, and Special Collections (MASC) http://libraries.wsu.edu/masc*

## Port Gamble Mills - 1889

E.G. Ames, Esq.
Port Gamble, W.T.

Dear Sir:

As Assistant General Manager of the Puget Mill
Company's Business on Puget Sound, Division I,
your headquarters shall be at Port Gamble, W.T.

You are expected to assist the General Manager in
the Supervision and management of Division I of
the Puget Mill Co. Business System. Which includes
all the General Business of the Company on Puget
Sound, Financial, General, Improvements, Building
and the Policy of the Company to be followed Etc. ...

You will be expected to keep a sharp lookout over
all property owned and managed or controlled by
the Company and report direct to the General Manager as often as required and circumstances make
necessary. ...

You are to see to it that all persons under your con-
trol are competent for positions they fill and if not
you are to take such steps as are necessary to supply
their places with men who are.

Yours respectfully,
General Manager

*University of Washington Library, Special Collections*

E. G. AMES.

General manager of the Puget Mill Company and its
associate institutions, one of the vice presidents of the Seattle National Bank and connected with many of the industrial concerns of the city and the Northwest.

19

E.G Ames, of the Puget Mill Company, located at Port Gamble, is an enthusiastic lumberman. He came from the state of Maine and knows how they prize Puget Sound spar timber cut there. He believes in letting all the world know of its excellence, so he informed an officer of the Washington World's Fair Commission the other day that if he was told how long a flag staff could be transported to Chicago he would supply the staff free at all cost. From this staff will float a flag in front of Washington's building.

*Pullman Herald.* Nov. 27, 1891

No man in all Seattle has larger business connections than E. G. Ames, who is at the head of the Puget Mill Company, with headquarters in Seattle, but with the mill plant across the bay. From a producing standpoint his concern has few, if any, equals hereabouts and as business manager and business director he gives Seattle the advantage of the business with which he is connected. The company owns a great many business blocks in Seattle and owns the Puget Sound Tugboat Company, which runs a line of steamers up and down the Sound, thereby affording another avenue for bringing wealth to the city.

It is said of Mr. Ames that he is always willing and ready to do anything that looks like it will give the Queen City a boost. Despite the fact he is at the head of one of the largest business institutions in the Northwest, he is always affable, pleasant and approachable by anyone having business with him.

*Seattle Republican.* Dec. 30, 1910

## Any Reduction Is Unjust

On the withdrawal of the Canadian lumbermen from the conference, the American lumbermen proceeded to express their views without reserve regarding the question of withdrawal of the duty; and it was the unanimous opinion of all Americans present that any reduction of the present lumber tariff would be unjust and contrary to the interests of the American lumber industry; but it was agreed that if the question of lumber tariff could be settled and taken out of politics for a long term of years, we would not impose a 20% reduction.

I think I voice the sentiment of the lumbermen of Washington, Oregon and California by suggesting that the reduction of 20% on rough lumber be considered the ultimatum of the American members of the joint high commission to their Canadian associates; and that no concession be made on dressed lumber or on small lumber, such as laths, staves, clapboards, pickets, shingles, etc.

I am informed that the United States sells to Canada annually about $80,000,000 worth of goods, wares and merchandise, simply because conditions favor our market; and that we buy of them about $45,000,000 worth annually for the same reason, leaving a balance of trade in our favor of $35,000,000. On account of this balance of trade and the desire to offset it with lumber, etc., instead of cash, the Canadian lumbermen ask the American people to remove its protection from its greatest industry, and open our great market to Canadian competition. Is not this a great hardship on a single industry with 45 per cent of the cost of its product labor, particularly when the Canadians have everything to gain and we all to lose?

I have heard it strongly intimated that the Canadian position is "Free Lumber or No Treaty." If that is so, let it be "No Treaty."

Yours respectfully, E.G. Ames

*The Seattle Post-Intelligencer.* June 9, 1899

*The Seattle Star.* Sept. 9, 1916

22

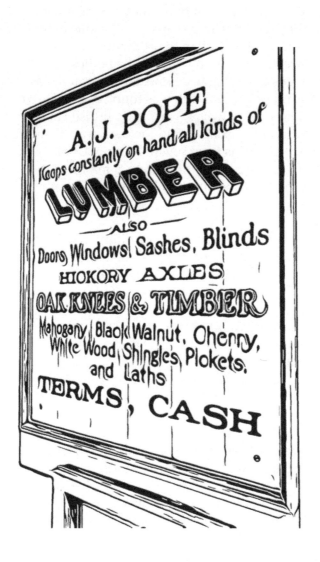

# A Foul Murder

On Thursday afternoon last information was received by Justice Dwelly, of Port Gamble, that two squaws were lying dead on the beach near Big Spit, on Hoods Canal, a few miles above Port Gamble. Mr. Dwelly sent an Indian to bring the bodies down to Gamble. The Indians returned with but one of the bodies, which showed no bruises, or signs of having been murdered. Search was immediately made for the other body, which was found near where the first was picked up. This one, however, was badly bruised about the head, as if beaten with a club or bottle, and the neck was scratched and torn, showing fingerprints as from severe beating. Upon searching in the vicinity for some clue to the murderers, a man was found on Big Spit, who gave the name of John Flaherty, and was taken into custody on suspicion.

This Flaherty is a sort of vagabond or tramp, who has been loafing around Port Gamble for a month or two, living on clams and what he could steal. On being questioned he stated that early on in the morning of the previous day, he had started up the beach to dig clams for his breakfast, but before he got to his destination he came across the camp of five men on the beach who were asleep. In the camp he found two bottles of whiskey and a loaf of bread, which he stole, abandoning the idea of digging clams, and started back down the beach. He had not proceeded far, before he met the two squaws, subsequently found dead. He gave the squaws a drink out of one of the bottles of whiskey, and he also gave them the other unopened bottle. They all three then proceeded back to the camp of the five men on the beach. These men were timbermen, and men that had been working around logging camps a little. One of the squaws presently started out into the woods a short distance to procure some water and was followed by a man named West. He stated, however, that he only followed her about twenty yards, but his pipe was picked up about fifty yards from the camp.

Warrants were issued for the arrest of all six of the men, and the trial and inquest lasted three days. Sufficient evidence could not be obtained to fasten the guilt upon anyone, and on Saturday afternoon the Coroner's jury brought in a verdict that the two squaws came to their death by being fouly dealt with by a party or parties to them unknown.

It came out in the evidence, however, during the inquest that the man Flaherty had furnished the Indians whiskey, he having confessed the same and that he had also committed larceny, some articles that were stolen from a resident of Port Gamble having been found in his possession. He confessed to the larceny, and said he would return the articles, which consisted of a suit of clothes and some other things, if the court would be lenient with him. The man West, before-mentioned, was also found to have sold liquor to Indians on the reservation commonly known as Boston, about a month or two ago. They were both arraigned before Judge Dwelly on Friday. Flaherty on a charge of selling liquor to Indians and grand larceny, and West on a charge of selling liquor to Indians. They were both convicted, and their bail fixed at $1,000 each to appear at the next term of the District Court. Failing to give bail, they were committed to the custody of the sheriff.

*The Seattle Daily Intelligencer.* June 5, 1878

## Chasing Contraband Chinese

Port Gamble, July 28. - [Special.] A steamer is reported to have landed thirteen Chinese near Port Gamble on Tuesday night. Inspector Coblentz and two deputies were here today searching. They have arrested three Chinese without certificates. None of the contraband Chinamen have yet been found.

*The Seattle Post Intelligencer.* July 29, 1892

Built in 1916 as millsite office, the museum, currently located on the lower floor of the general store, was designed in 1972 and opened in 1976 housing an abundance of historical items from Port Gamble and the sawmill.

*www.portgamble.com/museum*

General No. 4
October 18, 1911

Messrs. Pope & Talbot
San Francisco, Calif.

Sirs:

We sent you by Stmr. "Shana-Yak" eleven packages of furniture as follows:

| | |
|---|---|
| 1 | Lounge, crated. |
| 4 | Chairs, " |
| 12 | Chairs, " (2 per package) |

These are for Mr. Cyrus Walker and are shipped as per instructions from Mr. W.H. Talbot. We will send another lot of household goods for Mr. Cyrus Walker by Stmr. "Fairhaven."

Yours respectfully,
PUGET MILL COMPANY

*Port Gamble Museum*

February 27, 1912

Messrs. Pope & Talbot
San Francisco, Calif.

Gentlemen:

We are shipping the following packages on Stmr.
"Tiverton" for Mrs. Cyrus Walker:

3  Crates with 6 Mattresses.
3 Trunks; bed cloths and pillows.
2 Crates containing 3 brass bedsteads.
1 Box containing 6 bed rails.
1 Box containing glass doors for book cases.
10 Packages in all

We are sending you one trunk key herewith.

Yours respectfully,
PUGET MILL COMPANY

*Port Gamble Museum*

31

## POST OFFICE

Port Gamble's first community hall was built in 1869 as a dance hall and church. The present structure was designed in 1907.

The first floor had space for a doctor's office, a dentist's office, a barber shop, telegraph office, and post office. The auditorium on the second floor served as a meeting room, athletic venue, theater, movie house, and dance hall.

Letter No. 40
December 22, 1917

Puget Mill Company
Port Gamble, Washington

Gentlemen:

We have just been advised that the application of the Puget Mill Company for an agency to sell War Savings stamps at Port Gamble has been accepted and our appointment confirmed by authority of the Secretary of the Treasury.

SHOW YOUR PATRIOTISM

*You Can Command Their Respect by Doing Your Bit*

**Buy War Savings and Thrift Stamps**

We are informed that various posters and other literature advertising the sale of Thrift Stamps and War Savings Certificate stamps will be sent us in the near future, and when received we would like to have them posted in conspicuous places so that the attention of all employees can be easily attracted.

We believe that the plan, as adopted by the Government, in making it possible for the individual of small means to help in the prosecution of the war by subscribing in amounts best suited to his or her own resources, is an excellent one and we are convinced that it is our patriotic duty to do all in our power towards encouraging the sale of these stamps.

Yours respectfully,
PUGET MILL COMPANY

Letter No. 336
December 24, 1917

Puget Mill Company
Seattle, Washington

Gentlemen:

Our order was placed with the local Post Office this morning and as soon as we are supplied with the War Savings Certificates and Thrift Stamps we will put the matter before our employees and endeavor to get them to do their bit.

Yours respectfully,

PUGET MILL COMPANY

*Every Patriotic*
Man, Woman and Child
can now invest in the
United States Government
*as small a sum as 25 cents*

**Begin Today**

## Prices Fixed On Logs and Lumber

### War Industries Board Makes Maximum Rates For Fir Logs and White Pine Lumber

[By United Press]

WASHINGTON, June 22.—The war industries board today fixed a maximum price on fir logs and lumber produced in the Pacific northwest, also for yellow pine. Fir lumber prices were increased approximately $2.75 per thousand and yellow pine $4.80.

**Timber Industry Weathers Hard Times and Is Ready to Reap Long, Fat Harvest. Editor of West Coast Lumberman Gives Star His Reasons for Predicting a Handsome Revival in Trade**

Lumber is about the only commodity we know of that hasn't advanced in price 'because of the war,' or 'because of the strike,' or 'because of the demand,' or the 'short of labor,' or 'high price of material,' or something. Lumber is as cheap today as ever. And, there actually is a shortage of labor in some localities of Washington, and the price of saws, belting and other equipment for lumber manufacturing has gone up considerably.

We were able to cut more than we could carry away from the mill. The war caused a shortage in ships and that took away our carriers. Some lumber had to be sent by rail to the East.

Most of building will be with lumber because other building material has advanced in price. Steel and iron has gone 150 per cent higher and as a result the builders are turning to wood material.

Between 30 and 40 lumber-carrying vessels are now in the process of construction between Puget Sound and San Francisco. They will carry somewhere between 1,000,000 and 2,000,000 feet of lumber each.

*The Seattle Star.* Sept. 9, 1916

35

Built in 1903, the 55 room Puget Hotel was designed by Seattle architects Bone & Corner. Chinese cooks and waiters originally served businessmen and tourists.

During the years 1958-1961, the hotel housed workers constructing the nearby Hood Canal Bridge. Maintaining the structure became increasingly expensive. After the October 1962 Columbus Day storm blew shingles off the roof and rain drenched the interior, the hotel closed the following month and was demolished in 1963.

The Company prohibited gambling - and spitting on the floor - but the hotel was operated as a concession so wagering was allowed.

## Port Gamble Water Towers
## 1880-1885

The towers, each with a capacity of 50,000 gallons, supplied the hydrants located throughout the mill and community.

They were decommissioned in the 1960's after a reservoir was installed behind the Walker Ames House.

# 1875 Flag - 38 States

This flag was hand sewn by "Granny" Craig, wife of a Port Gamble foreman, and later given to James Kiefer, an early attorney for the Puget Mills.

Colorado was admitted as the 38th state on March 3, 1875. It would be another fourteen years before North Dakota was admitted as the 39th state on November 2, 1889. Following that: #40 South Dakota, #41 Montana, #42 Washington, #43 Idaho, #44 Wyoming, #45 Utah, #46 Oklahoma, #47 New Mexico, #48 Arizona, #49 Alaska and #50 Hawaii.

**St. Paul's Church**
3189 State Hwy 104 NE
Port Gamble, WA 98364

Built in 1878, St.Paul's Church was modeled after the Congregational Church of East Machias, Maine. The steeple bell arrived in 1879 as a gift from the San Francisco Pope & Talbot's officers' wives. Over the years the church has been a place of worship for numerous congregations, including Congregational, Baptist, Episcopal and, most recently (until 2005), Anglican.

View from Little Boston Road of St. Paul's Church and Olympic Mountains in background.

Dr. Atkinson invited the members of the Congregational Association of the Washington Territory, in accordance with a request of Dr. Lane, to be present at the dedication of the Port Gamble church, two weeks from tomorrow.

*The Daily Intelligencer*, Seattle. June 29, 1879

Rev. William Butler has been asked to take charge of the Congregational church at Port Gamble for the second year. Mr. Butler is pushing the church rapidly toward self-support.

*The Seattle Post-Intelligencer.* Dec. 7, 1891

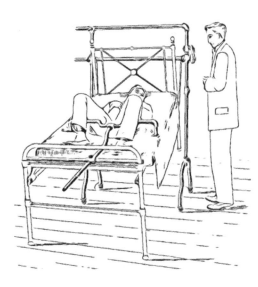

General No. 3
July 11, 1911

Messrs. Pope & Talbot
San Francisco, Calif.

Gentlemen:

In answer to your
General Letter #126 to the
Seattle Office, re accident
to J. Landis will say that
Mr. Landis left the Com-
pany's hospital at Port
Gamble after remaining
there one day, his present
whereabouts is unknown.

Yours respectfully,
PUGET MILL COMPANY

# Chapter III

# DANGER!

The next step in logging was the felling of the trees. This job was completed by extremely skilled men, known as fallers, who had to ensure the tree would fall in a specific direction without shattering the log. The fallers usually worked in pairs and, with the use of an axe, would first cut a notch into one side of the tree to help guide the direction of the tree when falling.

Most trees were notched a few feet up from the bottom of the tree except for the trees that were in the path of a potential railroad line. Two springboards, made from maple, were then notched into the timber and stood on by the fallers while they cut trees down. The springboard, another invention made specifically for the West Coast, was necessary to get above the flare at the base of the tree.

The fallers, working together, then sawed toward the notch from the opposite side of the tree, driving wedges between their saw cuts, until the wedges would eventually help topple the tree in the direction of the notch. The fallers warned other lumbermen of falling trees with a booming shout of "TIMBER!"

Bass, Kalley, "THE HIDDEN HISTORY OF WESTERN WASHINGTON LOGGING CAMPS: ST. PAUL AND TACOMA LUMBER COMPANY'S CAMP #5, ca. 1934-1947 (2017) .

It is interesting to watch the men as they skip from log to log, balancing themselves with a pike pole here, and riding a rolling log there, and occasionally missing a foothold and plunging a leg or perhaps half of their body into the water ere they can save themselves.

All of this to the amusement of the other drivers. Often their work is very hazardous as they toil with peavey and pike pole at the base of an overhanging mountain of logs in an effort to break a jam.

*Bonners Ferry Heald,* December 18, 1909

George Brady, a logger working in Bernard's camp, was drowned Saturday, while assisting to start some logs out of the boom. He went on a log without calks in his boots and fell, catching onto a small log; it turned over with him and he sank to the bottom. Joe Bernard saw Brady fall into the water and plunged after him, but was seized with cramps and was rescued with difficulty.

*Aberdeen Herald,* April 17, 1902

All workers must wear heavy-duty boots that cover and support the ankle and are water repellent in wet conditions. Workers who walk on trees, logs, or boomsticks must wear sharp caulked boots (or the equivalent). In ice, snow, mud, rocky terrain, or other conditions that render caulks ineffective, workers must wear heavy-duty non-slip boots. Workers who operate chainsaws must wear cut-resistant foot protection.

OREGON OSHA: *Yarding and Loading Handbook, July 2010*

CAULKS (calks, chalks): Heavy leather boots containing numerous steel caulks or spikes to promote secure footing.

**Leg Badly Crushed.** Nels Tyberg, while working at the Tyberg logging camp on the Lewis and Clark was seriously injured yesterday evening. He was alone at the time of the accident, but from what could be gathered from his brother afterward, it seemed that he was pulling at a log which slipped and crushed his right leg below the knee. He was hurried to this city and placed in St. Mary's hospital where the leg was amputated at an early hour last night. His condition is reported to be serious.

*The Morning Astorian.* (Astoria, OR) March 3, 1907

C.A. Walsh, employed in Adams & Costello's logging camp on the Chumstick, about twelve miles from town, was brought to Dr. Hoxsey's hospital last Thursday evening suffering from a fractured skull and spinal injuries, the result of being hit by a log rolling down the mountain side. He died Saturday at 11 o'clock and was buried on Sunday in the Leavenworth cemetery.

*The Leavenworth Echo.* (Leavenworth, WA) Sept. 25, 1908

**Logging Camp Injury.** August Besio, a Finnish employee of the Tsell Seppanen logging camp on Beaver Creek received a bad cut above the right knee Thursday afternoon. While at work he stepped from a bank some ten feet high and fell on his axe, gashing the flesh badly and splitting the bone. He was brought to Astoria at once for medical treatment.

*The Morning Astorian.* (Astoria OR) March 3, 1907

**Another Logging Injury.** Frank Dixon, an employee of the Button-Benninger logging camp was brought to the Eugene hospital Friday evening in an unconscious condition, suffering with a wound on the head, which was caused by a limb striking it while felling a tree. He is in a dangerous condition and the physicians will probably resort to trephining to relieve the pressure on the brain caused by indentation of the skull or hemorrhage. An unfortunate circumstance is the fact that no one knows where Mr. Dixon is from, so that his relatives, if he has any, can be communicated with.

*Daily Capital Journal.* (Salem, OR) August 28, 1905

48

Logging is dangerous. Injuries have been common and often fatal. Because loggers work in remote areas medical care is not readily available so even minor accidents can be deadly. Those who died in the woods were often referred to as moving on to "Section 37, where there was no brush, the ground was level, the rigging small, with a good place to rest and a cook whose specialty was apple pie with lots of cinnamon."

772 logging fatalities were reported in 1992-97, 70% from contact with trees and logs.

Eric F. Sygnatur, an economist in the Office of Safety, Health and Working Conditions, Bureau of Labor Statistics, provided the following grim report in an article titled *"Logging is Perilous Work"*:

Timber resources come at a price. Each year, between 100 and 150 loggers lose their lives and many more suffer non-fatal injuries. Loggers face a risk of fatal work injury approximately 27 times greater than the average for all occupations.

Trees post a number of hazards to loggers. Wind, structural irregularities in the tree, wet or sloped terrain, and structural failures within the tree such as heart rot, splits, breaks and cracks may cause the tree to fall at unexpected times in unexpected directions. Felled trees can become entangled in other trees or, less obviously and more commonly, broken tree limbs can be caught in nearby trees where they dangle capriciously, often falling onto unsuspecting loggers. The latter scenario is so common that hanging limbs are often referred to as "widow makers." Falling trees can also hit overhead power lines and telephone poles, or vines and other dense vegetation, resulting in erractic falls, fires, or entanglement. "Fish-tailing" trees sweep a large surface area as they swing sideways, and "mousetraps" sometimes occur when a felled tree strikes another, perhaps concealed log, which in turn strikes the logger. Even when the tree is settled it poses dangers when limbs become locked or bent. Loggers who cut those limbs must guard against slingshot effects, which can throw large limbs up to 50 feet.

Some 65 percent of logging fatalities occurred as a result of being struck by falling objects, most of which were trees and logs. Various types of non-roadway vehicular accidents, includng those caused by tractors and skidders, accounted for 7 percent of fatalities; loggers crushed or struck by rolling logs accounted for 5 percent; and falls from trees, 2 percent.

*Compensation and Working Conditions.* Winter 1998

According to a 1987 study, the average age of loggers with severe injuries, most often head trauma, was 34 years. If the injuries were not fatal, they often required long hospitalization and permanent disability.

*The Epidemiology of Logging Injuries in The Northwest.* Holman RG, Department of Surgery, Harborview Medical Center, Seattle, Washington  Olszewski A, Maier RV, The Journal of Trauma, 31 Aug 1987.

# CASEY JONES. THE LOGGER.

Come, all you woodsmen, if you want to hear
about a Washington logger who had no fear.
He knew his duties and made no mistake;
He chopped down trees and shoved 'em in the lake.
He was a modest logger, all unknown to fame;
He worked for the company just to get a name.
But if heroes are rewarded as their dues demand,
He is logging off timber in the promised land.
As the whistle blew each morning at half past four
Casey left his wife at the cook-house door,
Picked up his peavy and started down the track;
Never had a notion that he wouldn't come back.

The skid-roads were slippery, the cable wouldn't work;
Engine got to bucking and pulling with a jerk.
When logs came a-jamming, Casey he just said:
"We'll get them in the water, or we'll all be dead."

The logs started down the skid-road hill;
Casey jerked the whistle with an awful thrill.
The engineer knew by the whistle's moans
That the man on the wire was Casey Jones.
The logs coming 'round the first turn of the road,
And sweeping down the hill made a heavy load;
The haul-back broke with a whirr and hum,
And Casey Jones departed for kingdom come.

Whatcom Museum

"I am sorry," said Casey, just before he died,
"There's a few more camps I haven't tried."
The hook-tender said, "What haven't you seen."
"Why I've never been at Bellingham nor at Aberdeen."

Mrs. Casey in the bunkhouse spoke with much regret,
Of the troubles she had had since she and Casey met.
"Go to bed, children; he was a gay deceiver,
The next dad you get is going to be a shingle weaver."

-Aberdeen Logger. 1913

| Category | Job Titles | Wages (1939) |
|---|---|---|
| Management | General manager, logging superintendent, foresters, logging engineer | |
| Office | Timekeeper, stenographer, bookkeeper | |
| Camp Kitchen | Cook, waiter/waitress, dishwasher, flunky | $216 - $67 per month |
| Logging Operations Support | Blacksmith, blacksmith assistant, welder, saw filers | $7.70-$5.42 per day |
| Other Support Staff | Bedmaker, drag saw man, bull cook | $75-$85 per month |
| Timber Felling | Cruiser, faller, bucker, brush piler, brush burner, bull bucker, windfall bucker | $9.47-$6.32 per day |
| Yarding Crew | Hooktender, rigging slinger, choke setter, choke hold diggers, chaser, donkey puncher, loading punk | $7.83-$5.00 per day |
| High Lead Logging | High riggers | $10.20-$6.32 per day |
| Log Transportation | River rat, skid greaser, bull wacker | $9.47- $6.97 per day |

**Melton, Ray. 1939** *The Lumber Industry of Washington: Including Logging, Sawmills, Shingle Mills, Pulp & Paper, Specialties, Distribution.* **National Youth Administration of Washington, Tacoma, Washington.**

Note: $1.00 in 1939 = $18.50 in 2019

# GLOSSARY OF LOGGING TERMS

**Blow Down**. A tree felled by natural causes such as the wind.

**Buck**. Cut tree into specified lengths after it has been felled to more easily transport.

**Bullcook**. Boy who performs various chores around camp, including cutting wood for fuel and sweeping bunkhouses.

**Calks**. Lumberman's preferred footwear; high-topped, steel-spiked usually leather boot that helped give the lumberman steady footing on a fallen log.

**Choker**. Small piece of cable used to attach logs to the yarding system such as the skidder.

**Choker Hole**. A hole dug underneath a log to allow a choker to be placed around the log.

**Cold Deck**. Reserve of logs to be moved at a later date to ensure year-round income.

**Cruiser**. A forester or logger who estimates the amount of profitable timber, usually done by walking stands.

**Flunky**. Cook's assistant who often waits on tables.

**Gut Robber**. A camp cook who has received negative reviews from lumbermen.

**Landing**. Mostly flat ground where logs are yarded, to be loaded onto train or log truck for transportation to a lumber mill.

**Log Booms**. A barrier placed in a river or a lake that was designed to collect and corral floating logs timbered from nearby forests.

**Silviculture**. The planting, treatment, and management of a timberland usually completed by an employee known as a forester.

**Skidroad**. Path that logs are pulled on either by animals or specialized machines in later days.

**Spar Tree**. Tree used as the highest anchor point in high lead cable logging. The spar tree was selected based on height, location, strength and lack of rot all of which were needed in order to withstand the weight and pressure required. After a spar tree was selected a climber would remove the tree's limbs, top the tree, and fix several cables around. The spar tree has now been replaced by portable towers, called Yarders.

**Springboard**. A light and flexible piece of wood that is inserted into a notch in the tree to be used as a platform for fellers to stand on while felling the tree.

**Timber Beast**. A rough, tough, and ill-mannered lumberman.

**Tin Pants**. Waterproof clothing primarily worn by lumbermen in the Pacific Northwest.

**Widow Maker**. Dead limb hanging on a tree above a logger.

# *Chapter IV*

# SOCIETY

PORT GAMBLE. July 1. - What proved to be the society event of the season took place last night in the form of a grand ball given by Kitsap Lode, No. 96, Knights of Prythias. The hall was prettily decorated with flags, evergreens, swords, shields, etc., and reflects great credit on the committee attending to that part of the work. Music was furnished by Prof. Christian's orchestra from Port Townsend. Ice cream, cake and lemonade were served during the evening. Dancing was kept up until an early hour in the morning. The various committees performed their work in a very creditable and efficient manner.

*The Seattle Post-Intelligencer.* July 2, 1893


PORT GAMBLE. March 16. - A grand ball was given last evening at the hall, under the auspices of Prof. Aker's dancing classes, and proved to be one of the most enjoyable events of the season. The hall was tastefully decorated with flags and evergreens. Refreshments were served at midnight.

*The Seattle Post-Intelligencer.* March 15, 1895


PORT GAMBLE. July 2. - Thursday evening witnessed the most charming ball that has taken place in a long time. It was given by Mr. Kenneth Stewart. Several of the ladies of the Shakespeare Club worked for several days decorating the hall and last evening their efforts were exhibited, very much to their credit. The hall never looked prettier. The music was furnished by a Seattle orchestra. Dancing continued into the wee small hours.

*The Seattle Post-Intelligencer.* July 4, 1897

**Society at Port Gamble**

The church here last Sunday night had a very enjoyable and interesting song service, the pastor turning the entire evening into the service.

The apprentice boys on the English vessel Drumcraig gave a very interesting and enjoyable entertainment Thursday evening, consisting of select readings, music, both vocal and instrumental, and recitations.

The masquerade ball, the event of the season, was given in the Port Gamble town hall March 24. The hall was beautifully decorated for the occasion. The costumes were magnificent, representing ye olden style of British, French and Spanish courts. Music was furnished by Marotta of Seattle. The grand march, representing forty-five couples, was led by Mr. K. Stewart and Miss Lana Konlowski. Dancing continued to until 4 a.m. A dainty luncheon was served by Mr. D.A. Daggert.

*The Seattle Post-Intelligencer.* April 2,1899

## Drumcraig

A four-masted iron barque built in 1885 in Liverpool, England.

## House Party at Port Gamble

Port Gamble. April 24th. - Miss B.E. Kimble charmingly entertained a few of her friends at her residence last Saturday evening, the occasion being her birthday anniversary. Progressive whist was the game of the evening.

*The Seattle Post-Intelligencer.* April 25, 1897

# Do you play Whist?

"Whist, then, delightful Whist, my theme shall be,
And first I'll try to trace its pedigree,
And shew what sage and comprehensive mind
Gave to the world a pleasure so refin'd :

"*Ah Sir !*" said Talleyrand, once to a young fop who had boasted of his ignorance of "whist." "*What a sad old age you are getting ready for yourself !*" The strategy born of the battle-fields of green baize has ere now helped to capture kingdoms of the earth. A profound knowledge of whist carries with it a whole college of learning. Where is the game of skill with cards that has kept closer company with the march of culture than "whist" in its various stages of development during the past three hundred years? But this is no whist treatise. America is the adopted home of the game, New Haven herself a notable whist-center, remembrances that may excuse rambling enthusiasm.

Here are all the fitting necessaries of "whist" if you play or would learn. Also of most other popular card games.

**WHIST SCORE CARDS.** For Progressive Whist. Buy now for next winter at this price. These are printed on excellent quality of card. Thursday price 7c. doz. 50c a hundred.

*The New Haven Connecticut Daily Morning Journal and Courier.*
May 20, 1897

## Entertainment at Port Gamble

The entertainment given at Port Gamble March 16 was a pronounced success, as was prophesied when it was known that Miss Mills and Miss Robinson were the prime movers. The evening's entertainment opened with an instrumental solo by Mr. Willie T. Thompson, who surprised his many friends by his proficiency.

A children's play in 14 acts entitled "Beautify and the Beast" was then rendered. The cast was as follows:

Zemri, the merchant ..........    Arthur Platt
Azor, the beast    ..........    Carry Gove
Zemri's daughers:    ..........    Beauty ( Mamie Gove), Annie (Minnie Best), Lolo (Nettie Taylor)
Queen of Fairies    ..........    Lina Platt
Fairies, Imogen McKay, Beatrice Fetterly, May Storrs and Lizzie Kimball.

All the parts were well taken, but worthy of special mention are Minnie Best, who is quite a talented little actress, and Carry Gove, who as the Beast was hideous, and as the Prince Restored charming. The stage decorations were artistic, and the garden scene was especially admired. The Oriental costumes were picturesque in the extreme. The excellent music furnished by Miss Abbie Drew was appreciated by all. Port Gamble should be proud of the talent presented by her young folks.

*The Seattle Post Intelligencer.* March 24, 1889

*Chapter V*

# PARANORMAL

# Walker-Ames House

Built in 1889, the largest house in town and unoccupied since the mill's closure in 1995.

Reportedly one of numerous locations in Port Gamble of recurring paranormal activity, i.e. not explained by what is known about nature and the world.

Evening *Ghost Walks* are offered during the fall months. Visitors are encouraged to bring a flashlight and clothing for the weather.

"Cameras, meters, etc. are welcome."

*www.portgambleparanormal. com*

63

Although the last human residents left in 1995, the four story Walker-Ames house reportedly remains an active location for paranormal activity.

"As you walk through the house, pay attention to your emotions and how you feel."

Pete Orbea, Host & Guide, Port Gamble Paranormal

"There are so many different kinds of activities in this house."
Pete Orbea

# THE ACHING VOID

*By Duncan M. Smith*

OH, what did they do for diversion,
　　And how did they pass time away,
And what was the topic, I wonder
　　Of gossip by night and by day;
What was there to furnish excitement,
　　And how did they get on at all
Or manage to pass through a season,
　　Before they invented baseball?

It must have been mighty dry picking
　　When no one was winning three straights.
It may be the boys had a wrestle
　　Or mixed in a hot game of quoits.
In watching the curve of the horseshoe
　　And seeing just where it would fall.
They passed a wet day with the blacksmith
　　Before they invented baseball.

They sat round the drug store at checkers
　　Or maybe took chances on chess.
Or mayhap they only matched pennies
　　The dullness to partly suppress.
And sometimes, when life got too dreary,
　　They'd go to a show in a hall.
There must have been oceans of blankness
　　Before they invented baseball.

They had to go forth and fight battles
　　Or argue on points of the creed;
They had to fare forth with their weapons
　　To places where coons might be treed;
They had to fight bulls and run horses
　　Or curry their nags in the stall
To keep up a semblance of interest
　　Before they invented baseball.

*The Rock Island Argus.* June 13, 1912

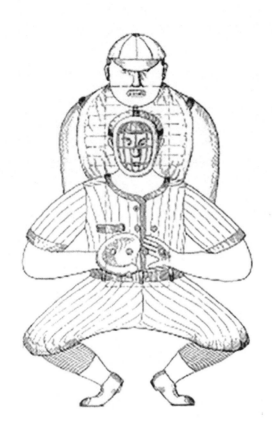

*Chapter VI*

# BASEBALL
# "THE GAMBLES"

A bat-and-ball game with some semblance to baseball can be traced to the 14th century.

A. G. SPALDING IN 1879.

Albert Spalding, he of considerable fame as a pitcher, manager and executive before co-founding A.G. Spalding sporting goods company (now a subsidiary of Russell Brands), believed the American game was similar to the colonial game of "one old cat."

Fervent followers claim it was their man Abner Doubleday who "invented" the modern-day baseball in Cooperstown, New York in 1839. And none other than Spalding did credit Doubleday for placing players in approximately the same position as they are today, albeit then 11 in number rather than today's 9.

Historical debates aside, there is no argument that baseball is firmly ingrained into American history and culture. The first officially formed club was The Knickerbockers of New York in 1845. The National League was formed in 1876, the American League in 1901. The World Series first occurred in 1903, with the Boston Americans of the American League defeating the National League's Pittsburgh Pirates.

There were a number of local teams around the Puget Sound during the late 19th and early 20th century, including the "Gambles" of Port Gamble.

# Base Ball Game

Port Gamble, beside her many other orders and societies for mutual benefit and amusement, now boasts of a base ball club. For the past two or three months the boys have been very industriously engaged in clearing a piece of ground back of the town, and now, in what was once a "bowling wilderness," there is a very credible base ball field. The following is the score of the first game of the two nines, and considering the condition of the ground and the boys not yet having their hands in it, it is a very credible amateur score, which we are sure will be greatly improved the next game, as the material is here for a number one club: "Live Game" 65 run - 27 outs. "Gamble Nine" 63 runs - 27 outs. Umpire: Honorable George W. Dwelly. Scorer: Mr. Wm. Calkins.

*The Daily Intelligencer.* August 27, 1876

# Base Ball Rules for 1877

Although the base ball season has hardly opened yet, we publish the following, which will no doubt be perused with much interest by all lovers of the "manly sport": "Among the changes in the code of rules for this year are the following: The size of the base is to be increased from 12 to 15 inches square. The home plate is to be brought into the diamond, the sides of the plate forming a portion of the foul lines. The second good ball after two strikes is to be called fair, after the manner of the amateurs. All dead balls, which are unfair, are to count against the pitcher, and toward helping the batsman to a base on called balls. Umpires are to be allowed to enter the field during the progress of the game. Fair fouls will not be allowed. If a player strikes at a ball plainly with the intention of not hitting it, he shall be declared out. Earned runs are not to be reckoned in scoring. If a ball when struck hits a base runner the latter shall be declared out."

*The Lewiston Teller.* January 27, 1877

## Bud Horton Gets A Good Offer

"Bud" Horton, the pitcher who piloted the Port Gamble baseball team to the front rank this summer and who is recognized as one of the best all-around players in the state, will probably play professional ball in Louisville or one of the Southern cities next season. He has received offers from Elmer Smith, who expects to have a team in Louisville next season, and from Ollie Beard, who used to captain the Spokane League team.

Horton has a host of friends in baseball circles on the Sound and all of them wish him success, even if the ranks of good ball players in this section are weakened.

*The Seattle Post-intelligencer.* Sept. 22, 1894

## Port Gamble beats Hadlock
## The Rubber Between The Teams Played At Port Townsend

The Port Gamble and Hadlock baseball teams met at Port Townsend last Sunday to battle for supremacy, the former coming out on top.

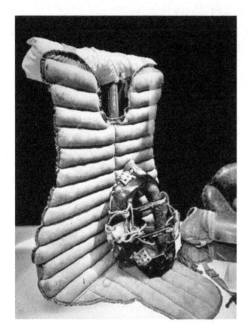

The teams had crossed bats twice during this season, each scoring a victory on its own diamond, so it was decided that the rubber should be played on neutral ground, and Port Townsend grounds was selected.

The players were escorted out to the park by the Key City band, and found a moderately large attendance anxious to witness the game.

Chet Dawson, of Port Townsend, was chosen umpire, and though his decisions may have been in one or two instances questionable, there was no kicking done by the players themselves.

The Gambles, by their bulldog grit and dogged perseverance won the game, which, in spite of a few errors and some ragged fielding, was full of excitement from start to finish. The final score was Gamble 15, Hadlock 14.

*The Seattle Post-Intelligencer.* August 10, 1892

Port Gamble General Store & Café

Butcher & Baker Provisions

Scratch Kitchen

The Artful Ewe and The Artful Ewe II

WISH Mercantile

Olympic Outdoor Center

Port Gamble Guest House

Tango Zulu Imports

Quilted Strait

Port Gamble Theater Company

OhSweetBrew

The Painted Lady

Gamble Cover Dahlias (Seasonal)

# *Chapter VII*

# RETAILERS

On Friday last the mill company's store at Port Gamble was destroyed by fire, causing a loss of about $80,000 to the company. The amount of insurance is unknown.

*Vancouver Independent.* December 9, 1880

Letter No. 312
November 24, 1917

Puget Sound Mill Company
Seattle, WA

Gentlemen:

Will you kindly inquire of the proper authorities if it is necessary for us to get licenses to sell food stuffs at Port Gamble and Port Ludlow. If each store would be considered separately and deliveries of food stuffs to the Company are not included, our sales would not amount of $100,000.00; but if the sales of both places and goods delivered to the Company are merged into one account, our sales would amount to more than $100,000.00.

If you will attend to this matter promptly, you will greatly oblige.

Respectfully yours,
Puget Mill Company

# Puget Mill Company General Store

**1853**

**2019**

## Port Gamble General Store and Cafe
32400 Rainier Ave NE
Port Gamble, WA 98364
Phone: 360-297-7637
*www.portgamblegeneralstore.com*

75

## Morrill Pope House

Built 1900-1901 in Port Ludlow for the supervisor of the mill.
It was barged to its present location in Port Gamble after 1929,
replacing the John Seavey house built in 1870.

## Tango Zulu
32239 Rainier Avenue NE #361
Port Gamble, WA 98364
Phone: 360-297-3030
*www.tangozuluimports.com*

## Michael S. Drew House

Built in 1860. The residence of the Company's timber agent and reportedly the largest timber owner in Washington.

## Wish in Port Gamble
32220 NE Rainier Ave.
Port Gamble, Washington 98364
Phone: 360-297-4114
*www.facebook.com/wishinportgamble*

## The Artful Ewe
32180 Rainier Avenue NE
Port Gamble, WA 98364
Phone: 360-643-0183
*www.theartfulewe.com*

Located in the shadow of the town's twin water towers, this 1903 building was originally the Company's store for locally raised meat and vegetables. It was later remodeled into a garage after the market moved into the store building in 1916.

## Butcher & Baker, Provisions
4719 NE State Highway 104
Port Gamble, Washington 98364
Phone: 360-297-9500
*www.butcherandbakerprovisions.com*

"A locally sourced farmhouse restaurant, butcher shop and
bakery offering small batch provisions and dining."

This structure was erected in 1903, one of the last built in Port Gamble. Pope and Talbot leased the space to a private operator, ensuring much-needed service without taking on the responsibility of managing the business. The canopy and sign were added in 1971.

## Quilted Strait
32280 Puget Way NE
Port Gamble, WA 98364
Phone: 1-855-GOQUILT (Toll Free)
*www.quiltedstrait.com*

This building was originally a stable for horses, but by the 1920's automobiles had replaced horses for transportation prompting its conversion to a garage. It later became a commercial site, presently occupied by Quilted Strait, featuring 4000 bolts of sewing cottons and an extensive collection of threads for stitching, embroidery and wool work.

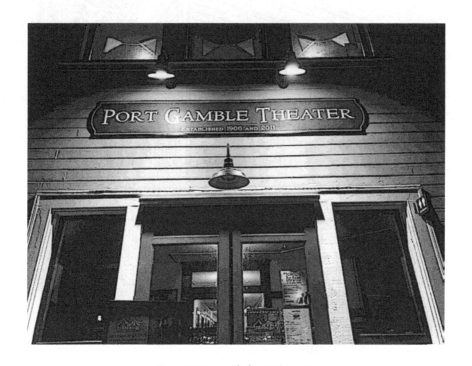

## Port Gamble Theater
Established 1906 and 2011
4839 NE View Dr.
Port Gamble, WA 98364
Phone: 360-977-7135
*www.portgambletheater.com*

The Port Gamble Theater continues the historical tradition of fine performances. The 2020 season's planned shows include: "Sarah Plain and Tall," William Shakespeare's "The Tempest," "Steel Magnolias," and Rodger's and Hammerstein's "Cinderella."

## The Painted Lady
32319 NE Rainier Avenue, Port Gamble, WA 98364
Phone: 360-265-1069
*ktladi2@gmail.com*

*"Listen to the Whispers and Giggles of the House. Come step back in time."*
Featuring a broad collection of vintage, artisan, repurposed, and rustic pieces.

The house was built by the Company to attract and retain the resident physicians who lived there over a long period of time. It likely served both as hospital and home to the town's resident physician until sometime prior to 1929, when the hospital was situated closer to the mill.

The Puget Mill fire hall, now the
Olympic Outdoor Center.

# Olympic Outdoor Center
32379 Rainier Ave.
Port Gamble, WA 98364
Phone: 360-297-4659
*www.olympicoutdoorcenter.com*

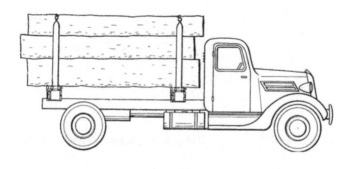

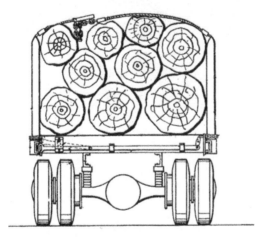

*Chapter VIII*

# INVENTIONS
# &
# INVENTORS
## 1887-1941

# Combined Band and Circular Saw Mill

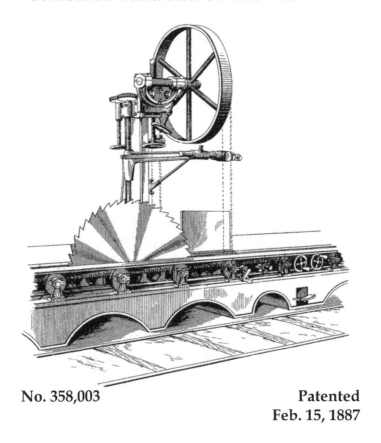

No. 358,003

Patented
Feb. 15, 1887

Our invention consists of a combined band saw and circular-saw machine or mill, and particularly in the construction and arrangement of the frame, arbors, pulleys, guides, etc., hereinafter set forth, by which we are enabled to use either saw at will, the two saws operating in the same plane, and consequently requiring but one rack-bench or log-carriage, one gage, etc., and needing no adjustment of these parts in changing from one saw to the other.

It is well known to those engaged or interested in the manufacture of lumber that, owing to its greater thickness, a circular saw cuts a wide kerf, and consequently wastes more lumber or produces fewer planks or boards from a given log than a band-saw, and, further, that lumber cut with a circular saw requires much deeper planing or dressing to remove the marks of the saw-teeth than lumber cut by a band-saw. On the other hand, a circular saw possesses advantages in the matter of speed and in other particulars, and is almost essential for slabbing, squaring logs, sawing crooked knotty lumber, and various other purposes.

**Edward White Turner and Jabez Reynolds**
**Inventors**

# Lumber Carrier

No. 448,766

Patented
March 24, 1891

This invention relates to wood-sawing, and is more especially a saw-mill appliance or log carrier adapted to convey logs from the points where the trees are felled to the saw-mill or to other suitable points; and the object of the invention is to provide an improved device of this character.

Alfred T. Kelliher
Inventor

# Log Splitter

No. 508,221

Patented
Nov. 7, 1893

The object of this invention is to construct a steam splitting machine for splitting logs, a splitting ax attached to one end of the piston rod and to be operated by the end thrust of said piston.

Another object is to combine the steam cylinder, piston rod and ax with a rope and toggle tongs in such a manner that when the piston rod ascends the ax will be raised and the log be raised up to be mounted upon the splitting block, at the same time.

**W.E. Hill**
**Inventor**

# Saw

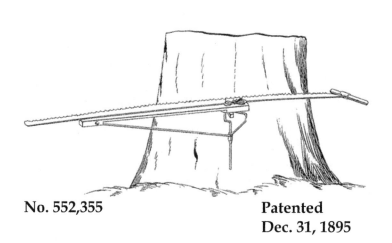

No. 552,355

Patented
Dec. 31, 1895

The object of the invention is to provide a new and improved saw-support, which is simple and durable in construction, and more especially designed to conveniently hold a cross-cut or other saw in proper position to permit a single individual to saw down a tree, no matter how large its diameter.

The invention consists of a saw-table held on a bracket mounted to turn on a shaft journaled on spikes adapted to be driven in the tree.

A.J. Deetz
Inventor

# Sawing Machine

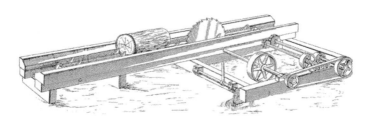

No. 672,498                    Patented Apr. 23, 1901

The object of the present invention is to improve the construction of sawing-machines and to provide a simple and comparatively inexpensive one adapted for cutting up logs of short lengths and designed more especially for enabling knotted and crooked logs, which are usually left in a forest to rot owing to the difficulty of splitting them with an ax, to be readily cut into cord-wood.

**A. Tothill**
**Inventor**

# Lumber Sorter's Toe Cap

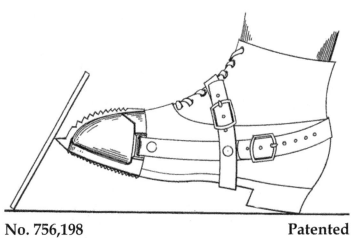

No. 756,198

Patented
April 5, 1904

The objects of my invention are to provide a metallic covering for the toe which will protect the foot-gear of persons engaged in handling and measuring large quantities of lumber, such as lumber-sorters, and specially lumber in the rough, and to make the cap with a spur at the tip and a serrated upper surface, by means of which the user can easily engage the lumber, and to provide means for properly securing the cap in position upon the foot as against the strains of such usage.

**Robert P. Adams**
**Inventor**

# Ax & Saw

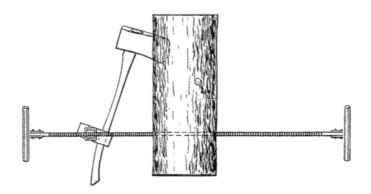

No. 880,412

Patented
Feb. 25, 1908

This invention relates to means for cutting or sawing logs or timber. The object of the invention is to produce a support or guide for a saw which can be readily attached to a log or timber with ordinary tools.

**Levi Smith**
**Inventor**

# Ax

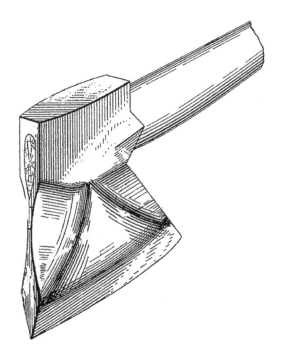

**No. 910,763**

**Patented
Jan. 26, 1909**

This invention relates to axes and has for its object to provide a comparatively simple and inexpensive tool of this character which will effectually cut or sever logs, trees or other timber with a minimum expenditure of energy on the part of the operator.

A further object of the invention is to provide a hollow ground ax having a cutting blade or bit the welding edge of which is provided with a row of perforations adapted to receive the metal when the bit is welded to the head or poll of the ax.

**H. Yeatts**
**Inventor**

# Locomotive for Logging

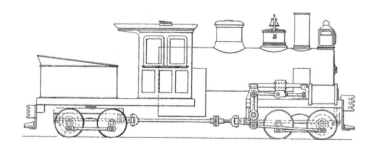

No. 923,564

Patented
June 1, 1909

My present invention relates to locomotives, and particularly to locomotives designed for use on rough and uneven roadbeds, such as are encountered in logging and similar operations. Railroads laid for use in such connection are constructed of comparatively light rail and heavy grades and sharp curves are apt to be of frequent occurrence, since the expense involved in their elimination would be unwarranted. These conditions impose, it will be obvious, peculiar requirements upon a locomotive designed for use on such track, chief among which are high traction power and flexibility with comparatively light load on any of the wheels. No great speed is required or desirable.

J.R. McGiffert
Inventor

# Log Hauling Truck

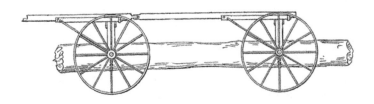

No. 1,230,131                          **Patented**
                                    **June 19, 1917**

This invention relates to log hauling trucks. The object of this invention is to construct an improved form of log lifting and transporting vehicle. By means of the arrangement of parts which embody the subject matter of my invention, I am enabled to cause the forward pull of the team which will haul the loaded vehicle to elevate the log from the ground. Thus, the device does away with all the mechanism which is ordinarily necessary for lifting the log from the ground into that position where it must hang or be supported when the logs are supported in transporting position.

J.S. Davis
Inventor

# Log Loading and Unloading Grappel

No. 1,429,161

Patented
Sept. 12, 1922

T his invention relates to new and useful improvements in load handling devices and particularly to devices for handling loads of logs.

In handling pulp wood logs, the logs are loaded on a sled or truck, and a chain passed around the logs and secured thereound. This consumes time. When the logs are to be lifted from the sled or truck and deposited on a car, it is necessary to remove the chain from the logs. This also consumes time, as well as labor.

It is the particular object of the present invention to provide a device whereby the use of chains is rendered unnecessary, the logs being loaded on the sled in the usual manner, and when the logs are to be removed and lifted to a car, by means of a crane or derrick, the entire load can be grasped, lifted from the sled, and quickly released when deposited onto the car.

**Otto Newlin**
**Inventor**

# Logging Truck

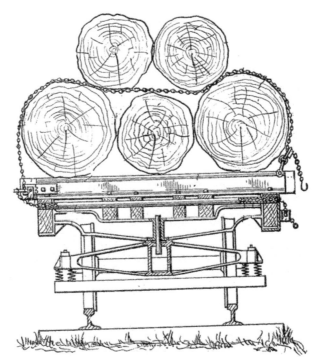

No. 1,512,771

Patented
June 27, 1923

Our invention relates to logging trucks and the like, and the object of our invention is to provide efficient means for securing the logs in place on the truck, and which means are so arranged that they may be released with safety to the person handling the truck.

A further object of our invention is to provide means of the character mentioned, which are simple and compact in construction, and may be easily applied to standard trucks and cars, and are adapted for withstanding severe service.

We attain our objects in combining with a logging truck, and the like, a log securing means comprising a pivoted, vertically movable pin on one side of the truck, a wrapper chain fastened at one end to the opposite side of truck and provided with an eye at its free end for securing on said pin; a trip chain, extending across the truck, provided with an eye at one end for securing on said pin, and means for securing the opposite end of the trip chain to the truck. The trip chain functions temporarily to hold the pin against being lifted by the strain of the wrapper chain, and the devices are so arranged that the means provided for securing said opposite end of the trip chain are located on that side of the truck opposite to that from which the logs will be discharged. Hence, the person handling the truck is out of danger during the releasing of the logs. All he does is to release said opposite end of the trip chain, so that the pin will be free to rotate and be lifted by the strain on the wrapper chain, which permits the link of the latter to slip off the pin, and thus releases the logs.

C.R. Lawyer, Et Al
Inventor

# Automatic Releasing
# Hoisting Device

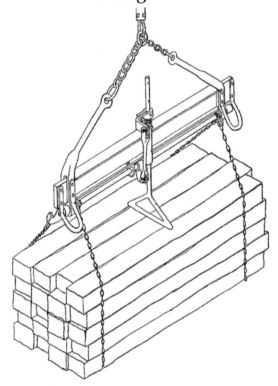

No. 1,862,312

Patented
June 7, 1932

This invention relates in general to hoisting apparatus and more particularly to a hoisting device provided with an improved mechanism for automatically releasing the load carried by the device when the load is lowered to a support.

In the prior art it is customary to hoist a load by passing two chains under the load and attaching the ends of the chains to two hooks which are held in spaced relation by a spreader member which in turn is supported from the hoisting cable of a crane. When the hoisting cable is raised the load will be lifted by the chains, and when the load is lowered to rest it is necessary that the ends of the chains be manually unhooked in order to disconnect the load from the hoisting device. This method of releasing the load carried by the hoisting device is hazardous, particularly when the material transferred is in the form of ties, logs, or timbers, because there is great danger of the load toppling over and falling upon the person who unhooks the chains.

A.L. Koszky
Inventor

113

# Logging Tractor

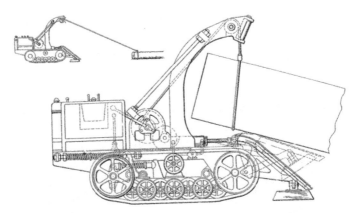

No. 1,987,688

Patented
Jan. 15, 1935

This invention relates to logging equipment and more particularly to a logging tractor including special equipment for skidding, yarding, transporting and other handling of logs; the machine being in the nature of a rapidly mobile power plant eminently suited to use in rough and heavily timbered country for the rapid handling and transporting of heavy logs and especially designed for a novel system of selective logging.

The principal object of this invention is to provide a tractor and equipment for the above stated purposes including an integral crane of the high arch type and a cable winding drum for the skidding, yarding and supporting of the logs for transportation and having also an auxiliary support associated with the tractor frame and adapted to be adjusted into use when needed for the purpose of extending the effective wheel base of the tractor and to thereby prevent tipping up of the tractor under heavy pull transmitted over the arch.

It is also an object of the invention to mount the auxiliary support in such manner and to so connect it with the power plant of the vehicle that it may be mechanically adjusted into and from functional position. Also, to provide automatically adjustable ground engaging supports for the outer end of the leg to adapt it to use on uneven ground.

It is another object of the invention to provide a skidding apron in connection with the auxiliary support useful in drawing logs up into the arch, and also for the support of logs while being transported.

**Frank H. Lamb**
**Inventor**

# Log Roller

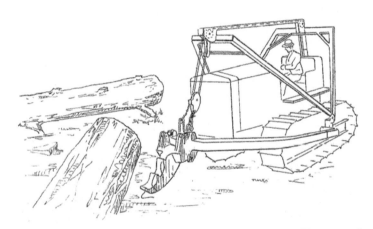

No. 2,235,913

Patented
March 25, 1941

Before entering into an explanation of this invention, it will be understood that when logging timber of a considerable size, it is the duty of the fallers to fell the tree, buck it in required lengths and cut off the limbs on the exposed surface. This is called limbing three sides or the top and both sides of the tree. Obviously, the "knotter" is unable to cut the limbs on the other side. When the logs are moved to the landing for loading, they not only skid hard but tear up the skid trails and landings and the loading crews are consequently delayed by waiting on the "knotters" who are called on to cut off the remaining limbs as they become exposed. To roll these logs over and knot them in the woods is a time and cost saver. This has been done in the past by using a swamp hook and cable attached to the Caterpillar. However, this requires two men on the ground and it is hard work climbing around through the brush.

The main object of my invention is to provide a mechanical log roller which performs its work with only the Caterpillar operator for man power and by means of which it is possible to roll a log any desired amount or push it for skidding with the expenditure of a minimum amount of time and effort on the part of the crew and equipment.

The second object is to construct a log roller which is merely an attachment for an ordinary track laying tractor whose log engaging jaw can be so positioned and manipulated as to obtain any desired rolling and positioning action.

**W.H. Beane**
**Inventor**

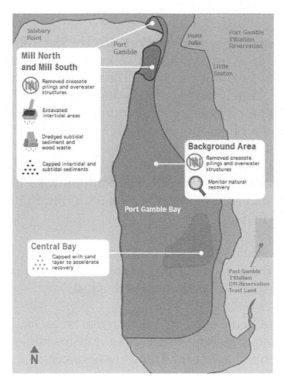

*[Source: Washington Dept. of Ecology.*
*Publication No. 17-09-062 April 2017]*

# *Chapter IX*

# RESTORATION

Pope & Talbot, Inc. used the Port Gamble Site from 1853 to 1995. Log rafting occurred within a 72 acre area along the western shore of the Bay beginning in 1974. The mill shut down in 1995 and the log rafting largely ceased at the same time. In 1997 the landfill area was leased for log storage and sorting, wood chipping, marine research and other light industrial activities.

The sawmill activity, operation of two chip barge loading facilities and log-transfer facility, sawmill emissions, in-water log rafting and storage areas, and creosote treated pilings all contributed to contamination at the Mill Site.

In 1998 the Washington State Department of Ecology notified Pope and Talbot of the potential listing of the Mill Site on Ecology's Confirmed and Suspected Contaminated Site List.

Ecology identified eleven potential source areas, including a petroleum product storage area, former transformer locations, wood treatment/painting area, and drum storage areas.

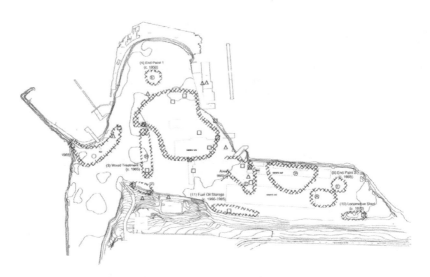

[Source: Washington Dept. of Ecology, Agreed Order No. DE 15448]

A Consent Decree for remedial action at the Port Gamble Bay and Mill Site was signed in December 2013 between the principal parties: State of Washington, Department of Ecology (Ecology), Pope Resources LP (PR) and Olympic Property Group LLC (OPG).

The 110 page document incorporated an October 2013 Port Gamble Bay Cleanup Action Plan.

STATE OF WASHINGTON
KITSAP COUNTY SUPERIOR COURT

STATE OF WASHINGTON,
DEPARTMENT OF ECOLOGY,

NO.

13 2 02720 0

Plaintiff,

CONSENT DECREE

v.

PORT GAMBLE BAY

POPE RESOURCES LP,
OPG PROPERTIES LLC.

Defendants.

## TABLE OF CONTENTS

PORT GAMBLE BAY                                    i
CONSENT DECREE

ATTORNEY GENERAL OF WASHINGTON
Ecology Division
PO Box 40117
Olympia, WA 98504-0117
FAX (360) 586-6760

Between 2002 and 2005, 26,310 tons of contaminated soil were excavated as interim remedial actions from the uplands area. Subsequent groundwater monitoring through 2016 confirmed that metal concentrations remained stable and were below natural background concentrations.

Between 2003 and 2007, 31,000 cubic yards of wood debris were dredged in the nearshore area adjacent to the sawmill.

*[Source: Washington Dept. of Ecology,Publication #17-09-066. October 2017]*

Between 2015 and 2017, attention turned to the in-water portion of Port Gamble Bay and Mill Site.

## BEFORE

8,592 creosote-treated pilings were removed, along with 77,297 cubic yards of contaminated marine sediments, 110,537 cubic yards of wood waste and contaminated sediment, and an acre (56,500 square feet) of overwater and derelict structures.

The cost upon completion was $2.4 million contributed by the State of Washington and $20 million by Pope Resources/OPG, LLC.

*Source: Washington Dept. of Ecology*

**AFTER**

The Olympia oyster seed is Washington's only native oyster. Historically, distribution encompassed between 4,000 to 5,000 acres of Puget Sound, but by 2011 the habitat had been reduced to about 155 acres representing only about 4 percent of the historic population.

A ten-year program was initiated by federal, tribal, state, local agencies and non-profit groups, including Washington Conservation Corps, to rebuild the breeding population through habitat restoration.

The project, carried out by the Puget Sound Restoration Fund, funded in part with $994,000 by the Washington State Department of Ecology, involved producing 5 million Olympia oyster seeds for outplanning in the bay, spreading shell over 9 acres of tideland, and assessing oyster growth, recruitment, and survival.

Spraying bulk shell off a barge at high tide.

Volunteers helping spread shells.

In April 2015 the Washington State Department of Ecology provided $297,000 to transplant approximately 24,000 eelgrass (Zostera marina) shoots into four plots over 2 acres along the south shore of Port Gamble Bay.

Eelgrass provides important habitat for herring, juvenile salmon and crab, and is an indicator of the health of the maritime environment.

A 2016 followup study conducted by the U. S. Department of Energy found high mortality of the transplanted eelgrass, which it attributed, in part, to late season planting, a storm shortly after planting and turbidity of the water generated by the remedial dredging and excavation which was ongoing at the time.

*Port Gamble Bay Eelgrass (Zostera marina) Restoration Monitoring Final Report Port Gamble S'Klallam Tribe Natural Resources Department.* https://bit.ly/36ea7Z2

*Chapter X*

# LOOKING FORWARD

# Port Gamble Redevelopment
## September 2019 Proposal
*www.portgamble.com/masterplan*

*www.kitsapgov.com/dcd/Pages/Port_Gamble_Redevelopment.aspx*

Olympic Property Group on behalf of Pope Resources, the project applicant, is proposing redevelopment of the Port Gamble site.

The 318.7 acre site, comprised of three main areas including a mill site along the waterfront, a town site on the bluffs above the mill site, and an agrarian area which lies to the southwest of town.

Proposed redevelopment of Port Gamble could ultimately contain approximately 152,000 square feet of new commercial uses, a 100 room hotel and approximately 270 residential units (including 28 existing residences), with over 100 acres of open space.

**Master Plan Alternative 1**

- Full development on mill site
- 100-room hotel
- 202,000-sf new commercial
- 265 new residences (293 total)
- Rural agritourism parcels
- 160-acres of open space
- Adjacent to 3,500-acre shoreline park

**Master Plan Alternative 2**

- Smaller mill site development
- 16-acres of waterfront open space
- 100-room hotel
- 80,000-sf new commercial
- 226 new residences (254 total)
- Rural agritourism parcels
- 160-acres of open space
- Adjacent to 3,500-acre shoreline park

**What will stay the same:**

- The historic homes, store, theater, church and business buildings will remain.

- Many acres of open space with large trees and wetlands will be permanently protected.

- Trail connections will get even better, with plans for a future shoreline bluff trail, a new beach access trail, trail connections to a Mountain Bike Ride Park and space for the County's future Sound to Olympics trail.

**What will change:**

- We propose to give up the heavy industrial zoning that currently allows a mill or manufacturing on the mill site.

- Instead, there may be homes, a hotel, some commercial or open space on the mill site. We want to create destination agritourism like a winery, cidery and farm-to-table experiences on the hill near the old Babcock farm.

- There will be new homes and businesses in town. Port Gamble has been slowly disappearing since the 1920s when the auto repair building was built, signaling the beginning of mill employees moving out of town and the gradual loss of Port Gamble's buildings. The grand Puget Hotel, the hospital, school, the four-story, 100-room hotel annex, and most of the homes are gone now.

- Port Gamble will no longer be a company-owned town. People will be able to buy a home, business or agricultural property.

- One of the first new property owners will be West Sound Wildlife Shelter, who care for our region's wildlife. They will have plenty of space for injured birds and mammals to recover before being released back to the wild.

*[Developer Statements]*
*www.portgamble.com/masterplan*

129

In 2011, the Port Gamble S'Klallam Tribe joined with Forterra (formerly Cascade Land Conservancy), Washington State's largest land conservation organization, and a large coalition of local and state agencies, businesses and community groups to create the Kitsap Forest and Bay Project, dedicated to the conservation of 6,700 acres of land and 1.5 miles of shoreline in North Kitsap County, much of which directly affects the health of Port Gamble Bay.

As a result of the group's efforts, in 2014 Kitsap County acquired 535 forested acres and 1.5 miles of shoreline along Port Gamble Bay. In December 2016, the County obtained an additional 1,356 acres of the Port Gamble Heritage Park. A year later, funded by $4 million in donations and grants, Forterra secured acquisition of more than 1,500 acres of the Port Gamble Forest, bringing the total of conserved acreage to 4,000.

The Port Gamble Forest includes 65 miles of public trails, accessible to hikers, runners, bicyclists, equestrians, and bird and animal watchers.

The following quote by Jeromy Sullivan, Port Gamble S'Klallam Tribal Chairman, is found on the Forterra website,

"Saving this land means that my children's children and generations beyond will be able to practice the ways of our culture, harvesting from the surrounding waters, and continuing to act as stewards to the same forest, land, and sea that connects them to their ancestors."

PORT GAMBLE S'KLALLAM
THE OFFICIAL NEWSPAPER OF THE PORT GAMBLE S'KLALLAM TRIBE  |  WWW.PGST.NSN.US  |  360-297-2646  | DEC 2019

## An Historic Agreement

*PGST and Pope Resources reach deal that includes land purchase, environmental conservation, and partnership in redevelopment of Port Gamble*

# Pope Resources, Port Gamble S'Klallam Tribe enter into historic land deal *Kitsap Daily News,* December 25, 2019

In December 2019, the Kitsap Daily News and the newsletter of the Port Gamble S'Klallam Tribe reported that following five years of discussions Pope Resources agreed to sell to the Port Gamble S'Klallam Tribe 937 acres of timberland, comprising approximately two-thirds of Pope Resources' timberland in Hansville, north of Little Boston.  Pope Resources will retain rights to additional timber harvest rights for up to 15 years.

The tribal newsletter reported that it was securing funding for the purchase of a conservation easement on approximately 18.4 acres and adjacent tidelands along the former mill site's shoreline in Port Gamble.  Pope Resources will also lease portions of its tidelands in Port Gamble Bay to the Port Gamble S'Klallam Tribe. The Tribe's plans include restoration and rehabilitation of ecological processes and conservation values with access to the public.

Made in the USA
Las Vegas, NV
16 December 2021

37957090R00075